The World of Transportation

Addition

Rann Roberts

Publishing Credits

Dona Herweck Rice, *Editor-in-Chief*; Lee Aucoin, *Creative Director*; Don Tran, *Print Production Manager*; Sara Johnson, *Senior Editor*; Jamey Acosta, *Associate Editor*; Neri Garcia, *Interior Layout Designer*; Stephanie Reid, *Photo Editor*; Rachelle Cracchiolo, M.A.Ed., *Publisher*

Image Credits

Teacher Created Materials

5301 Oceanus Drive
Huntington Beach, CA 92649-1030
http://www.tcmpub.com
ISBN 978-0-7439-0861-0
© 2011 Teacher Created Materials, Inc.
Made in China
Nordica.032015.CA21500127

Table of Contents

Getting Around on the Ground

For thousands of years, people traveled on foot. They carried their own things. Then people began to tame animals. They put loads on horses. In some countries, camels or elephants carried heavy loads.

In the early 1800s, people put wheels to work. The first bikes had to be pushed. The next bikes had pedals with wooden tires. Riding them was hard work!

Bicycle History

1817 **The first bicycle had to be pushed.**	
1860s **The Boneshaker was made of wood.**	
1870s **The High Wheel bike was all metal.**	
1888 **Bikes got air-filled tires.**	

The first rickshaws had wheels. They were pulled by a strong runner. You can still get a ride in a rickshaw in many big cities. But sometimes they run on pedal power.

Dogs also helped with **transportation**. They pulled sleds in places with lots of ice and snow. Many dog sled teams have been replaced by snowmobiles.

The first railway to move people and goods was built in England. It was 25 miles long. It took about 2 hours to go that far. That is about 12 miles per hour.

LET'S EXPLORE MATH

Over time, trains have gotten faster and faster. The chart shows how many miles 3 trains can travel each hour with stops. Study the chart. Then use **addition** to answer the questions.

Year	Name of Train	Miles in 1st Hour	Miles in 2nd Hour	Miles in 3rd Hour
1829	*Rocket*	30	20	35
1832	*American*	60	50	55
1934	*Zephyr*	110	100	105

a. How many total miles did the *Rocket* travel in 3 hours?

b. How many total miles did the *American* travel in 3 hours?

c. How many total miles did the *Zephyr* travel in 3 hours?

A lot has changed since 1825. There are all kinds of trains now. The bullet train in Japan can go 186 miles in just one hour. It can travel 372 miles in 2 hours. Now, that is fast!

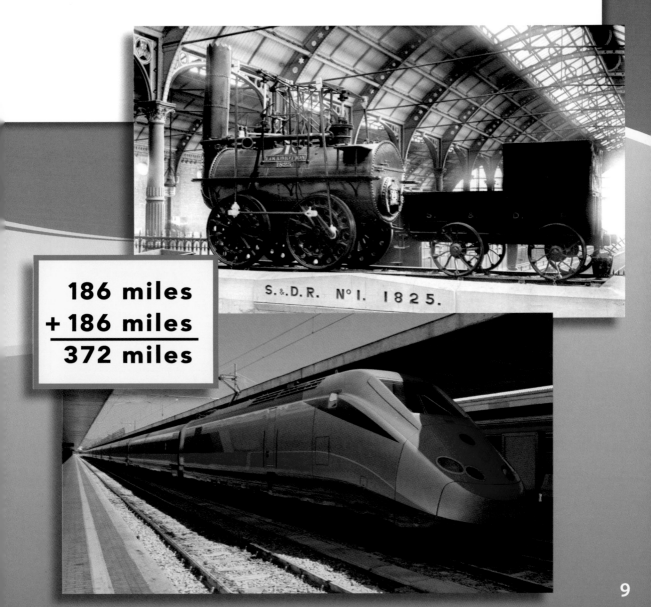

S. & D. R. Nº I. 1825.

186 miles
+ 186 miles
372 miles

Getting Around Above and Below the Ground

Most big cities have a system for getting places. A **rapid transit system** moves a lot of people from place to place. It is fast and makes a lot of stops.

Rapid Transit System	City
Subway	New York City Beijing
L or **Elevated**	Chicago
Metro	Paris Tokyo
Tube or Underground	London
SkyTrain	Bangkok Vancouver
Monorail	Seattle Sydney Moscow
Funicular	Hong Kong Cape Point Budapest

Some rapid transit systems are above the ground. Some move through **tunnels**. Some go above and below the ground. Some even travel under the water!

Rapid transit systems take you where you need to go. They are a fun way to get around!

LET'S EXPLORE MATH

The chart shows how long a train takes to get to 5 stops. Study the chart. Then answer the questions.

Stop	Time
Main Station to Center City	13 minutes
Center City to North View	11 minutes
North View to Park Place	20 minutes
Park Place to City Zoo	21 minutes
City Zoo to Bear Lake	14 minutes

a. How many minutes does it take to get from Main Station to Center City?

b. How many minutes does it take to get from Main Station to North View?

c. How many minutes does it take to get from North View to City Zoo?

d. How many minutes does it take to get from Park Place to Bear Lake?

Have you been to a theme park? You may have ridden on a monorail there. Some cities have monorails for their transit system. Riders get a good view!

If you need to go up a steep hill, you might ride a funicular. One car goes up the hill. The other car goes down. They balance each other on a cable system.

The longest train system in the world is the Trans-Siberian Railway. You can start in Moscow and go all the way to the Sea of Japan. It crosses one third of the globe. That's about 6,000 miles!

Moscow

Russia

Sea of Japan

The Trans-Siberian Railway was a big job. It took from 1891 to 1913 to build. That is 22 years!

Getting Around on the Water

Thousands of years ago, you could have sailed on a Chinese junk. These strong wooden ships still sail on the seas.

A much faster modern ship is the
hydrofoil. It goes so fast that it lifts up
out of the water. This one speeds down
a large river in China.

A freighter is a large ship. It moves goods around the world. Some large freighters even have cranes to lift off the cargo. This chart shows a trip that freighters take.

Los Angeles to Spain	Number of Days to Each Port
From Los Angeles to Tokyo	14
From Tokyo to Korea	2
From Korea through the Suez Canal	21
From the Suez Canal to Spain	10

The freighters travel slowly. They take many days to deliver the goods.

LET'S EXPLORE MATH

Study the chart on page 18. Then answer the questions.

  a. How many days does it take to get from Los Angeles to Tokyo?

  b. How many days does it take to get from Los Angeles to Korea?

  c. How many days does the whole trip take?

Taking a cruise can be a great vacation. A large cruise ship can hold 2,000 or 3,000 people. That's like a small floating city!

These 4 cruise ships hold from 101 to 3,114 guests. On which would you like to travel?

Name of Ship	Weight	Number of Guests
Spirit of '98	9,600 tons	101
Royal Princess	45,000 tons	1,200
Rhapsody of the Seas	78,491 tons	2,000
Adventure of the Seas	142,000 tons	3,114

A cruise ship may stop at many places, called **ports of call**. You can visit different cities or countries on 1 trip.

Getting Around in the Air

A large balloon with an **engine** is called an airship. An airship is filled with a gas that is lighter than air. The largest airship was the *Hindenburg*. It crashed in 1937.

Here are some interesting facts about the *Hindenburg* airship.

Length: 803 feet	**People in Crew:** 40
Diameter: 135 feet	**Passengers:** 40
Speed: 81 miles per hour	

Over the years, air travel has come a long way. Now you can take a short trip in a prop plane. Helicopters are used for travel and to help people.

Jet planes can travel long distances in a short time. The biggest jet is the Airbus 380. It has more than 500 seats!

LET'S EXPLORE MATH

Type of Vehicle	Speed
large helicopter	150 miles per hour
seaplane	140 miles per hour
Cessna jet	400 miles per hour

a. How many miles can a large helicopter fly in 1 hour?

b. How many miles can a large helicopter fly in 2 hours?

c. How many miles can a seaplane fly in 2 hours?

d. How many miles can a Cessna jet fly in 2 hours?

The fastest passenger plane was the Concorde. It could fly 4,500 miles in about 4 hours. That means it flew more than 1,000 miles per hour. But the Concorde was not safe enough to keep flying.

Do you dream of going to outer space?
The space shuttle can take you there.
It flies more than 17,000 miles per hour.
It carries a crew of 7 astronauts.

Some astronauts live and work in outer space for 6 months at a time. They live on the **International Space Station.**

What type of transportation would you like to try? Where would you like to go?

Transportation Collections

Marco, Juan, and Chris are friends. The boys like to collect different types of transportation vehicles. They each have a collection of model cars, model trains, and model airplanes. This Saturday, they decide to meet at Juan's house to play and trade vehicles. Use the chart below to answer the questions.

Name	Model Cars	Model Trains	Model Airplanes
Marco	45	11	20
Juan	21	10	32
Chris	33	14	13

Solve It!

a. How many model cars do they have in all?

b. How many model trains do they have in all?

c. How many model airplanes do they have in all?

d. Which type of vehicle is their favorite? How do you know?

e. Which type of vehicle is their least favorite? How do you know?

Use the steps below to help you solve the problems.

Step 1: Add together the number of model cars each boy has.

Step 2: Add together the number of model trains each boy has.

Step 3: Add together the number of model airplanes each boy has.

Step 4: Look at the totals to see which type of vehicle has the highest total?

Step 5: Look at the totals to see which type of vehicle has the lowest total?

Glossary

addition—the process of joining 2 or more numbers together to make 1 number called the sum

elevated—raised above the ground

engine—a machine used to move things

International Space Station—a place in outer space where astronauts live and work

ports of call—places visited by ships

rapid transit system—a railway for moving people around a city

transportation—a way to move people and things

tunnels—underground or underwater passages

Index

Let's Explore Math

Page 8:

a. 85 miles

b. 165 miles

c. 315 miles

Page 12:

a. 13 minutes

b. 24 minutes

c. 41 minutes

d. 35 minutes

Page 19:

a. 14 days

b. 16 days

c. 47 days

Page 24:

a. 150 miles

b. 300 miles

c. 280 miles

d. 800 miles

Solve the Problem

a. 99 model cars

b. 35 model trains

c. 65 model airplanes

d. model cars; answers will vary.

e. model trains; answers will vary.